Got Braces?

The Braces Cookbook 2

Comfort Food with a Gourmet Touch

Pamela Waterman and Amee Hoge

Mesa, AZ
www.theDiscoveryBox.com

ISBN: 978-0-9774922-3-7

Published by the Discovery Box
1955 W. Baseline Rd., Ste. 113-234
Mesa AZ 85202
480-897-3380   Fax 480-897-3379
www.theDiscoveryBox.com
www.BracesCookbook.com

Printed in Canada

Dedication

To Jack, Hilary, Gretchen and Jan,
for their love and support;
to Amee for the friendship that has grown
since that first day in the parking lot;
and to Brenda, who started it all.

— PJW

To all of my young chefs,
especially Katie, William, Ashley, and Alli;
playing with food in the kitchen with all of you
brings me great joy.

— ALH

Acknowledgments

To Lynn Schneider, founder of ArchWired.com, for great conversations

To the members of the Arizona Book Publishing Association, for sharing their wisdom from A to Z

To Angie DiMaggio, for expert photography advice and that "just do it" attitude

To Pam Paladin, for her creative approach to PR that makes work fun

To Connie Walker, for her sincere interest and objective view

To Lynn, Bill and Katherine Field, for "Field-Testing"

To Jeff White, Randall Black, Christine Gray, Mary Hunter, Alena Pacheco, Laura Robinson, and Dr. Adam Goodman, DMD, for feedback and encouragement

Cover design by Pamela Waterman and 1106 Design, Phoenix, AZ

Interior design by 1106 Design, Phoenix, AZ

Cover photo by Leasures Designer Portraits, Chandler, AZ

Interior photos by Amee Hoge, Your Culinary Companion, Mesa, AZ

Food styling by Amee Hoge, Your Culinary Companion, Mesa, AZ

Indexing by Shana Milkie, Ann Arbor, MI

— A portion of the proceeds from this book benefits Smiles for a Lifetime, a program that pays for braces and dental care for high school students.

Contents

Foreword

Congratulations, you got braces! Now, what on earth can you eat?

The realization usually sinks in quickly after the brackets go on: savoring a thick steak, gnawing on a slab of ribs, or tearing into a chewy panini will be challenging, if not downright impossible. For the next year or two, you'll probably want to cut your linguini and slice your burgers into manageable pieces. Most of your food choices will need to be soft and easy to chew. But that doesn't mean they will have to be boring.

Lucky for you, nowadays "soft food" doesn't mean your choices are reduced to mashed potatoes, soup, and smoothies. You can still enjoy a delicious variety of gourmet meals thanks to Pam Waterman and Chef Amee Hoge. A few years ago, Pam and her teenage daughter published **The Braces Cookbook: Recipes You (and your Orthodontist) Will Love.** This popular collection of recipes and tips was hailed as a lifesaver by braced people worldwide.

When Pam herself recently got braces, she decided to expand her repertoire to include gourmet soft food recipes for the discerning adult palate. In **The Braces Cookbook 2: Comfort Food with a Gourmet Touch,** Pam and Chef Amee (who trained at the French Culinary Institute in New York) have created 50 exciting dishes that you can dress up or down, depending on your time, energy, and preferences.

As an adult in braces, you're part of a growing trend. According to the latest statistics from the American Association of Orthodontists, more than one million adults in the US now wear braces! Coping with braces in the business world can be challenging, as I found out when I got braces at age 41. Business lunches and dealing with oral hygiene in the office and on the road can become cumbersome, but help is available.

In this book, Pam includes many tips and suggestions for handling these challenges. **The Braces Cookbook 2: Comfort Food with a Gourmet Touch** is a terrific resource for adults who want to straighten their teeth without missing the enjoyment of delicious food.

I'm sure you'll enjoy Pam and Chef Amee's new recipes, and that they will help to make your life more pleasant and flavorful while those braces do their magic on your smile.

— **Lynn Schneider**

Editor of ArchWired.com, The Website for Adults in Braces, and Owner of DentaKit.com, "Great Stuff for Braces & Beyond"

Introduction

As an adult, you want interesting, fun, delicious, or intriguing food options, sometimes all at once. At the same time, your braces-clad teeth may hurt, and certain foods could damage all those wires and brackets. **The Braces Cookbook 2: Comfort Food with a Gourmet Touch** steps in with the solution to this dilemma, offering 50 recipes for dishes that are easy on tender teeth yet go far beyond yogurt and applesauce. Most of the recipes are for main meals, the major concern of adults in braces, though you will also find ever-soft appetizers, braces-loving breakfasts and several divine desserts.

In developing recipes for today's adults, the authors combined their experiences to produce "real food from real ingredients." Pam, having cooked her way through both childhood- and adult- braces, and Chef Amee, known for bringing fresh ideas to everyday eating, kept the following thoughts in mind:

- Make the recipes easy to prepare from off-the-shelf ingredients, available at a mix of nationwide, mid-range and high-end stores
- Use standard amounts from packages and cans to avoid waste
- Use simple, pure ingredients without additives
- Avoid corn syrup whenever possible and ease back on total sugar

Pam developed the basic recipes to be comforting even on tender-teeth days, and to avoid being hard, sticky, chewy or crunchy. For each recipe, Chef Amee added her own gourmet touch, whether an extra ingredient, something spicy, an unusual garnish or a delightful suggested accompaniment. The choice is yours—enjoy!

The authors are happy to provide this variety of comfort foods in a single, convenient place. Savor eating once more with **The Braces Cookbook 2**, and for additional ideas, especially desserts, try the original **Braces Cookbook: Recipes You (and Your Orthodontist) Will Love** (Pamela and Brenda Waterman, 2006).

Soothing Tips for Difficult Days

Thousands of braces wearers before you have come up with their own ideas to make this process as comfortable as possible. Try these tips before, during and after an adjustment appointment.

For you:

- Take acetaminophen, ibuprofen or your doctor's recommended pain reliever one hour ahead of your appointment to get the medicine into your system.
- Be sure to tell the staff if you have a latex allergy. There are non-latex options for gloves, ligatures, chain-ligatures, mouth-guards and whatever else is needed.
- Drink or eat something very cold after an appointment; this delays the movement of your heat-responsive metal wires.
- Rinse with salt-water three or four times a day—this trick is enormously helpful during the first three days of braces.
- Lie down with cold washcloths resting on your cheeks.
- If something really feels as though it's poking or scraping, cover it with wax, then call and go into the orthodontist's. It **does** happen that a wire or hook may not have been placed quite correctly, and the technician can usually quickly adjust it to make a world of difference. Speak up!
- Hang in there. Yes, it will hurt for a while for the first couple of days, and after adjustments, but it's so worth it.

For your cooking:

- Try microwaving a frozen item instead of popping it in the toaster or oven (think frozen waffles—they definitely come out softer this way).
- Seal up casseroles and meat dishes with foil while cooking them in the oven—moisture will stay in the dish, and you'll avoid it becoming crispy on the top or edges.
- Eat leftovers! Many crunchy recipes soften up overnight in the refrigerator.
- Seal freshly baked items in tightly lidded containers—this really helps keep them soft. Or, add a slice of fresh bread to a sealed container of baked goods—the moisture will transfer to the cookies, bars, etc. and soften them up.

Easy Eating

Brown-bag lunches! Take-out dinners! Fast food! We all need them, so here are suggestions for making simple put-together meals, for home or on the road.

(* Items with an asterisk are particularly good for those first Difficult Days.)

Main Dish Foods

American, brie, and feta cheese; other cheeses when shredded

Burritos, with shredded meat and/or beans

Chicken—baked, barbequed or in nuggets, cooked until very tender

Chili*

Couscous

Crabmeat, flaked

Egg salad*

Fish—boneless, baked, and flaked in small pieces

Toddler meat sticks/turkey sticks/chicken sticks (they come in a jar in the baby-food aisle)*

Grilled cheese sandwiches, with crusts cut off

Vienna sausages (in a can)

Hot dogs, boiled and cut up

Macaroni & cheese, well cooked*

Meatloaf—very moist, with lots of breadcrumbs in it

Pasta—any kind, well cooked, with sauce*

Pot stickers (Chinese dumplings)

Ramen noodles*

Ravioli—canned or well cooked from frozen*

Rice—plain or flavored

Salmon—baked or poached

Soups*

Tacos—soft

Taquito roll-ups—microwaved, so they don't get crunchy

Tamales, canned

Tortellini, well cooked

Tuna salad

Yogurt*

(* Items with an asterisk are particularly good for those first Difficult Days.)

Breakfasts
Cream of Wheat hot cereal*

Eggs—boiled, scrambled, poached

Oatmeal hot cereal*

Pancakes

Waffles

Vegetables/Fruit
Acorn squash*—baked

Apples—cut into thin slices

Applesauce*

Bananas—ripe

Carrots—boiled

Cauliflower—cooked to be quite tender

Corn—cooked on the cob, but cut off with a knife

Grapefruit—ripe

Green beans, especially the tiny variety

Grapes—cut in half

Guacamole dip on pita bread slices

Mandarin orange slices

Pears—ripe or canned slices

Pear sauce, or any of the other new fruit mixtures*

Peas

Potatoes—baked, mashed*

Desserts
Cream pies

Flan custard

Ice cream, frozen yogurt, popsicles and sherbet (without nuts or candy chunks)*

Jello®*

Pudding—made from a box, or in individual pudding cups*

Rice cakes

Tapioca pudding*

Dining Out is Do-able

Think you're stuck at home with your braces, or doomed to carry a sack lunch everywhere? With a little creativity, your away-from-home eating can still be delicious and safe for your braces. Just remember to cut all food into smaller-than-usual bites.

Read on for do-able ideas.

In restaurants:

Tamales instead of tacos

Corned beef hash instead of steak, roast or pork

Sloppy Joes instead of hamburgers

Lasagna instead of pizza

Noodle dishes instead of thick pasta; you may be able to order them "well done"

Cooked vegetables instead of raw ones

Baked or mashed potatoes instead of French fries

Baked or steamed fish instead of fried fish

At parties:

Instead of eating hard crackers with a dip, see if there are bread slices and spread the dip with a spoon or small knife

Try potato chips instead of tortilla chips

Ask for a fork and knife to cut up finger food into individual bites

Offer to bring a dish that you know will work for you!

Braces in the Business World
Coping Techniques

One week after getting adult braces, Pam had an important conference to attend in New York City. At lunch the first day, what was on the menu? Large slabs of steak, ruffled spinach salad, strips of raw carrots and yes—hard rolls encrusted with seven types of seeds.

Eating out at business functions can definitely be a challenge for those in braces. When your teeth are sore, steak is not a great choice even when cut in small bits. If you have a choice, try a hamburger, and even then consider cutting it into quarters that are more easily nibbled. Try soups, seafood, vegetarian mixtures, soft chicken dishes, egg quiches, cooked vegetables, and pastas.

There's a difference between food that will break brackets and food that simply sticks a bit; the latter is just fine in the privacy of your home, but at business functions you may have to temporarily choose items not at the top of the healthy-eating list. You basically want to avoid having food take up residence in your front teeth, so try taking discreet bites slightly at the side of your mouth. White rolls instead of multi-grain versions will bypass the stuck-seeds problem, mashed potatoes can be temporarily quite filling, and cauliflower bits dipped into ranch dressing will leave less obvious traces than raw broccoli dipped into pesto sauce.

Two fantastic items to carry everywhere are a mirror and a tiny, self-covered spiral brush. Your orthodontist should give you the mirror as part of that little box with wax strips (essential for travel if a wire pops loose). With the mirror discreetly pulled out of a pocket, you can easily do a quick "teeth check." The brushes, about a quarter-inch-diameter and two inches long, come with a cover that becomes a handle—they are life-savers for coaxing stuck bits from between two brackets. Keep one in a pocket or purse, one in your desk drawer, and a few in a briefcase. Don't leave home without them! (See Websites, p. 120, for resources.)

Lastly, keep smiling! You're doing something great for yourself, and you just may inspire someone else.

Pantry and Tool Suggestions

Handy food items to stock:

In the freezer— Sweet bell peppers, chopped (buy them on sale)
Onions, chopped (prepackaged)
Celery, chopped
Chicken (boiled, diced, stored in 2-cup bags)

In the fridge— Garlic, chopped (buy it in a jar)
Onions, whole
Cheeses, shredded, in bags

On the shelf— Rice (white, brown, basmati, wild)
Pastas (angel hair, shell, orzo, rotini, twists)
Noodles (fine, medium, wide)
Couscous (plain and flavored)
Diced tomatoes, canned
Broth (chicken, beef, vegetable) (in a can or box,
or powdered to mix your own)
Beans (red, kidney, garbanzo)
Seafood (salmon, tuna, crabmeat)

Tool suggestions:

Food processor—works especially well on large pieces
Hand food-chopper—good for onions, sweet bell peppers,
soft nuts, etc.
Blender—the old stand-by for mixing fruits and liquids
Hand-held immersion blender—fantastic for an individual
smoothie
Kitchen shears/scissors—great for cutting dried fruit and
raw chicken
Fine strainer—they come in various sizes with handles
Pastry bag—for drizzling chocolate or adding whipped cream
Fish spatula—the metal kind is great for crumbling ground beef
Zester—for getting that burst of flavor from a lemon, lime
or orange
Grater—buy one with several sizes of holes
Grapefruit knife (serrated and curved)—handy for scooping
out fruit
Berry stemmer—saves your fingertips
Ice-cream maker—electric types are a real time-saver

Braces-Loving Breakfasts

Branberry Muffins

Thank goodness for frozen blueberries! They'll let you quickly stir up two dozen high-crowned muffins with a soft, break-away texture. Pam's mother perfected these treats more than fifty years ago. Keep them sealed in a plastic container for freshness, enjoy them with coffee or tea and grab a few in a bag for an on-the-go breakfast or snack.

3½ cups plain bran flakes
2 cups milk
3 eggs
½ cup vegetable oil
1 cup brown sugar
2 cups all-purpose flour
3 teaspoons baking soda
1 cup blueberries (frozen or fresh)

Preheat oven to 400 degrees. Bake for 21 minutes.

Grease cupcake pans for 24 muffins or line the pans with cupcake papers. In a large bowl, combine bran flakes and milk, and let the mixture sit for five minutes to soften the flakes. With an electric mixer, add the eggs, vegetable oil and brown sugar until well mixed. Gradually mix in flour and baking soda.

By hand, stir in the blueberries just until evenly mixed. The batter will turn a bit blue, but that's fine. Spoon batter into 24 muffin cups—this will pretty much fill each one to the top. Bake at 400 degrees for 21 minutes. Store in a tightly lidded container.

. . . .

Chef Amee's Gourmet Touch

Replace the milk with buttermilk and top the baked muffins with freshly grated nutmeg.

. . . .

Classic Sour Cream Coffee Cake

Pam makes this cake first thing every Christmas morning, carrying a family tradition into a third generation. It helps to let the stick of margarine soften for an hour at room temperature, but if you're pushed for time, just cut it into a dozen or so bits to speed up the mixing job.

½ cup (1 stick) butter or margarine
1 cup sugar
8 ounces sour cream
2 eggs
2 cups all-purpose flour
1 teaspoon baking soda
1 teaspoon baking powder
1 teaspoon vanilla

Topping:
  ¼ cup sugar
  1 teaspoon cinnamon

Preheat oven to 350 degrees. Bake for 45 minutes.

In a large bowl, with an electric mixer, blend the margarine and 1 cup of sugar until creamy. Add the eggs and sour cream and mix well. Add the flour, baking soda, baking powder and vanilla, and mix until smooth.

Grease a 9" round or square pan. Spoon half of the batter into the pan. In a small bowl, stir together the ¼ cup of sugar and cinnamon. Sprinkle half of this mixture over the batter. Spread the remaining batter in the pan, and sprinkle it with the rest of the cinnamon-sugar. Bake at 350 degrees for 45 minutes.

. . . .

Chef Amee's Gourmet Touch

Instead of a crumble topping, drizzle on an orange-almond glaze after it's been baked by combining the zest and juice of half an orange, ¼ teaspoon pure almond extract and ⅓ cup powdered sugar.

. . . .

Poufed Peach Cobbler

The fragrance is heavenly from this cobbler, a baked-fruit casserole from long-time Massachusetts friend Phyllis Leonard. Keep canned fruit on hand for quick preparation and scoop the mixture into glass dishes for an elegant dessert. On the rare occasion that the cobbler doesn't disappear in one sitting, it makes great leftovers. Just reheat on medium-power for a minute or so in the microwave.

¼ cup butter or margarine (softened)
½ cup sugar
2 teaspoons baking powder
¼ teaspoon salt
1 cup all-purpose flour
½ cup milk
1 (29-ounce) can sliced peaches (drained, but keep the liquid,
    about 1¼ cups)

Preheat oven to 375 degrees. Bake for 55 minutes.

In a large bowl, using an electric mixer, combine the margarine and sugar until well mixed. Beat in baking powder, salt, flour and milk until mixture is smooth.

Pour batter into an ungreased 3-quart casserole. Spoon the fruit over the top, then pour on the reserved liquid. Bake at 375 degrees for 55 minutes. Makes 6 servings.

....

Chef Amee's Gourmet Touch

Replace canned fruit with some in-season fruits such as berries, diced peaches or mangoes and sprinkle them with 1 to 2 Tablespoons of sugar for a simple syrup. Pour 1¼ cups water over the top.

....

Double-Scrambled Egg Baskets

These individual "bread-baskets" are a brunch-ready twist on serving scrambled eggs. Add your own mix-in touches such as grated cheese, sweet peppers or crumbled cooked bacon. The left-over bread crusts make terrific French-toast sticks the next day.

7 eggs total (use 2 then 5)
3 Tablespoons milk
Shortening for greasing pan
8 slices bread (whole-wheat is extra good)
2 teaspoons salt
1 Tablespoon margarine or butter
(optional: 3 Tablespoons grated mild cheddar cheese)

Preheat oven to 350 degrees. Bake for 15 minutes total.

Generously grease 8 cups of a 12-cup muffin pan, including the top surface around each cup. Cut crusts off 8 slices of bread (save them for another day). In a large bowl, whisk or stir together 2 of the eggs with the milk. With a fork, dip each slice of bread in the milk-egg mixture, coating both sides, then push one slice down into each greased muffin cup; make the middle touch the bottom, and have the edges stick above the rim. Let stand 5 minutes so that the bread fully absorbs the milk-egg mixture.

Bake the bread slices at 350 degrees for 13 minutes, then set them aside. Turn the oven up to 425 degrees. In a medium bowl, whisk or stir together the remaining 5 eggs, salt and any mix-ins you desire. In a medium-sized frying pan, melt the margarine or butter until sizzling, then add the 5-egg mixture and stir frequently until the eggs are fluffy but not browned. Scoop 2 heaping Tablespoons of scrambled egg into each bread-basket. If you'd like, sprinkle each with about 1 teaspoon of grated cheese. Bake at 425 degrees for 2 minutes. Makes 8 egg baskets.

. . . .

Chef Amee's Gourmet Touch

Add about ¼ teaspoon freshly ground nutmeg to the egg mixture. Top each egg basket with ⅓ cup diced sweet bell pepper and replace the cheddar cheese with squares of Swiss cheese.

. . . .

Raspberry Lemon Muffins

For a tart yet tender start to your day, serve these lemon muffins that cradle seedless raspberry jam. The secret to their moist, sponge-cake-like texture is yogurt. The extra-tart kick comes from the triple zing of yogurt, lemon juice and pure lemon extract, found in the grocery store where you buy vanilla.

1¾ cups all-purpose flour
¾ cup sugar
1 teaspoon baking powder
1 teaspoon baking soda
¼ teaspoon salt
1 (8-ounce) container plain yogurt
¼ cup vegetable oil
1 teaspoon lemon extract
1 Tablespoon lemon juice
¼ cup seedless raspberry jam

Preheat oven to 400 degrees. Bake for 17 minutes.

In a large mixing bowl, stir together the flour, sugar, baking powder, baking soda, and salt. In a small bowl, stir together the yogurt, vegetable oil, lemon extract and lemon juice. Add the lemon mixture to the flour mixture and stir until well blended. Batter is quite thick.

Line a muffin tin with 12 cupcake papers. Spoon batter to half-fill the papers. Press a teaspoon of raspberry jam in the center of each muffin; fill with remaining batter. Bake at 400 degrees for 17 minutes.

. . . .

Chef Amee's Gourmet Touch

Replace all-purpose flour with my favorite secret baking ingredient—whole-wheat pastry flour, about 1½ cups. Not only is it healthier, but it keeps baked goods moist longer. Also, replace plain yogurt with Greek-style yogurt sweetened with honey.

. . . .

Ever-Soft Appetizers

Hot Artichoke Spread

Prior to trying this recipe Pam was fairly convinced she didn't like artichokes. Not that she could remember having actually tried one; they seemed beautiful but just a bit too exotic. Fortunately, her adventurous California cousin Sarah Foss prepared this puffy baked appetizer and saved her from never realizing how delicious (and simple) this taste combination could be.

1 cup regular mayonnaise
    (Full fat version. This is not a diet recipe!)
1 cup grated Parmesan cheese (from a can or fresh)
¼ teaspoon salt
2 cans (13.75-ounces) artichoke hearts
    (Do not use the marinated variety)
(optional: ½ teaspoon paprika)

Preheat oven to 350 degrees. Bake for 30 minutes.

In a large bowl, stir together the mayonnaise, cheese, and salt. Drain artichoke hearts and cut them up into half-inch chunks or smaller. Stir artichokes into mayonnaise mixture.

Grease a 2-quart casserole. Spoon artichoke mixture into casserole. Sprinkle with paprika to add a little color. Bake at 350 degrees for 30 minutes or until slightly puffed and golden. Serve warm with pita bread or slices of a fresh baguette, crusts removed.

· ·

Chef Amee's Gourmet Touch

Add 8 to 10 fresh basil leaves, finely chopped, 2 to 3 teaspoons dried ground sage, 1 teaspoon of smoked Spanish Paprika and lots of yummy garlic, about 3 to 4 garlic cloves, finely chopped. This will jazz it up a bit!

· ·

Cherry-Chicken Salad Bites

Dried cherries are now as easy to find in the grocery store as raisins, a development that makes this variation on chicken salad a simple and delicious change of pace. When your braces come off, add ¼ cup of slivered almonds for extra pizzazz.

1 (12.5-ounce) can (or 1¼ cups) cooked chicken
½ cup (about 3 ounces) dried cherries, presoaked in hot water for
    10 minutes, then drained
½ cup (4 ounces) black-cherry yogurt
1 Tablespoon mayonnaise

Drain the chicken and break it up into a medium-sized bowl. Add cherries, yogurt and mayonnaise. Stir together well. If you have time, let the mixture sit in the refrigerator for an hour to absorb the moisture and flavors.

This serves up nicely in tiny scoopfuls on ruffled red-leaf lettuce, and is also excellent as a filling inside sliced miniature croissant rolls.

· ·

Chef Amee's Gourmet Touch

Add ¼ cup ground almonds and 1 to 2 teaspoons of dried mint leaves to add a little bit more color and texture to this scrumptious chicken salad.

· ·

Baked Stuffed Mushrooms

They must have coined the phrase "tasty morsel" for these tender and irresistible appetizers shared by Pam's world-traveler friend Cheryl Mezack. Two dozen small to medium mushrooms work well, but plan at least three per person.

1 pound (approximately) mushrooms* with stems,
    about one-inch in diameter (brown Baby Bellas
    have terrific flavor)
3 Tablespoons butter
1 Tablespoon minced parsley
½ cup grated Swiss cheese
1 egg, lightly beaten
½ to 1 teaspoon salt, to taste
⅓ cup seasoned bread crumbs
1½ Tablespoons butter for dotting

Preheat oven to 350 degrees. Bake for 20 minutes.

Wash and dry mushrooms. Remove stems and chop them finely. Sauté stems in a medium-sized frying pan in 3 Tablespoons butter for 4 or 5 minutes. Remove from heat, and add parsley, cheese, egg, salt and bread crumbs. Stir until well mixed.

Lay mushroom caps top-down in a lightly buttered 9" x 13" pan. Spoon some of the mixture into the hollow of each mushroom cap. Dot with butter. Bake at 350 degrees for 20 minutes. You can make them ahead of time, unbaked; cover and refrigerate, then uncover and bake as above.

*Buy 24 small to medium mushrooms. Mushrooms will vary greatly in size and weight; therefore, if your 24 mushrooms weigh more than 1 pound, adjust the quantity of filling accordingly. For example, if your mushrooms weigh a total of 1½ pounds, add another half-recipe of the filling mixture.

. . . .

Chef Amee's Gourmet Touch

Add 2 sprigs of finely chopped fresh parsley leaves to the filling. Add ⅓ cup of finely chopped onions and 2 to 3 chopped garlic cloves to the mushroom stems to sauté and cook according to instructions above.

. . . .

Miniature Crabmeat-Cucumber Sandwiches

These appetizers are quick to assemble yet make an impressive presentation on a tray. The thin slice of cucumber adds just a little crunch and is friendly to braces. It also helps keep the bread at just the right texture.

1 loaf "party" pumpernickel rye bread (often found at the
    deli counter, the little slices are just 2½-inches square)
1 large cucumber, about 8 inches long
2 (6-ounce cans) crabmeat, drained
3 Tablespoons mayonnaise
3 (4-inch x 8-inch) slices Swiss cheese
Paprika for sprinkling

Broiling time about 2 minutes.

On a large cookie sheet, lay out 24 slices of the bread (store the rest in your freezer for another time). Peel and slice the cucumber into 24 ¼-inch-thick slices; lay one slice on each piece of bread.

In a large bowl, stir together the crabmeat and mayonnaise until well mixed. Spoon a Tablespoon of the crab mixture onto each cucumber slice. Cut each slice of Swiss cheese into 8 approximately 2-inch x 2-inch squares, and place one cheese-square onto each appetizer. Sprinkle each open-faced sandwich with paprika.

Turn on the broiler of your oven. Place the cookie sheet under the broiler for about 2 minutes, until the cheese has started to melt.

You can assemble the appetizers, cover the pan with plastic wrap, and store it in the refrigerator overnight. Let the pan come to room temperature, remove the wrap, and broil just before serving.

....

Chef Amee's Gourmet Touch

Add 1 finely chopped Roma tomato and 1 teaspoon dried thyme leaves to the filling. If you are serving this for a special occasion, I recommend you serve it with a semi-sweet Italian wine such as a Moscato or Sangiovese.

....

Roasted Bell Pepper and Garlic Dip

Chef Amee developed this recipe as an appetizer, but Pam likes to make a meal from a bowlful. The texture is so creamy, it allows you to indulge in walnuts yet not wreak havoc with your braces. If you can find all the ingredients freshly grown, all the better.

1 bulb garlic (cut off the top, leave papery covering on)
3 large sweet bell peppers, any color, halved, with seeds
**   and white ribs removed**
1 Tablespoon vegetable oil (olive oil is best)
Pinch of salt
⅓ cup walnuts
½ medium red or yellow onion, peeled
1 Tablespoon dried parsley
2 Tablespoons lime juice
⅓ cup feta cheese, finely crumbled
1 teaspoon salt
½ to 1 cup sour cream, your preference

Preheat oven to 475 degrees. Bake for 20 to 25 minutes.

On a baking sheet, place both the garlic and the peppers cut-side down. With a paper towel or pastry brush, rub olive oil on the garlic top and the peppers' skins. Sprinkle with salt. Bake at 475 degrees until skins are very dark, about 20 to 25 minutes.

While the peppers and garlic roast, finely chop and combine the walnuts, onions and parsley. In either a food-processor or in a medium bowl, stir the lime juice and feta cheese into the walnut mixture; add the teaspoon of salt.

Allow the sweet peppers and garlic to cool. With a fork or knife, scrape the skins from the peppers, and squeeze each garlic clove out of its papery skin. Add peppers and garlic to food processor and continue to chop finely, or chop them finely on a board and stir them into the bowlful of the walnut mixture. Stir in sour cream until well blended. Spoon into a dipping bowl, and serve with torn pieces of fresh pita bread. Makes about 3 cups.

· ·

Chef Amee's Gourmet Touch

I love this recipe, so healthy, fragrant and fun to eat; pair it with an "earthy" Spanish red wine such as Tempranillo or garnacha.

· ·

Marvelous Main Meals
Beef • Chicken • Seafood • Pork

Modern Mulligan Stew

The tomato soup in this classic one-pot meal does a wonderful job of tenderizing the small cuts of beef. Allow two hours start to finish, though most of that time the stew takes care of itself.

2 pounds stew beef, cut in 1-inch cubes (for best results, buy a
    roast such as chuck, and cut it up yourself)
1 Tablespoon vegetable oil
5 medium onions, sliced
5 carrots, peeled and cut in one-inch slices
2 teaspoons salt
2 (10½- to 14-ounces) cans cream of tomato soup undiluted
2 soup-cans of water (divided)
6 to 8 red potatoes, cut in four pieces each

Cook on stovetop, about 1½ hours total.

In a Dutch oven or very large pot, cook the chunks of beef in the vegetable oil over medium-high heat for 5 minutes. Slice and add the onions and carrots, and cook for 15 minutes, stirring occasionally. Add salt, both cans of tomato soup and one (1) soup-can of water. Cover and bring to a boil, then lower the heat to a moderate simmer and cook covered for 30 minutes.

Add the potatoes, cover, and continue to simmer the stew for 45 to 60 minutes. Stir halfway through and add another soup-can full of water. You can always let it simmer longer—just check to see if the liquid needs a little more water. Makes 6 to 8 servings; recipe can be cut in half.

....

Chef Amee's Gourmet Touch

Replace red potatoes with hearty sweet potatoes for added flavor and nutrients. I also recommend "deglazing" the beef with 1 cup of a dry red wine such as a Cabernet Sauvignon or pinot noir to grab all of the flavors that seemed to have attached themselves to the bottom of your pan. This is done after the beef is nearly cooked and before you add the vegetables.

....

Wild Rice and Barley Stovetop Mix

Garden herbs, barley and an unexpected ingredient—raisins—make this one-pot meal both fragrant and hearty. It's also a great way to use up leftovers from a pot roast. Plan ahead a little, as the barley takes 40 minutes to cook; after that, everything heats together quickly. Try serving generous spoonfuls nestled next to lightly steamed green beans and hot croissant rolls.

**2 cups beef or vegetable broth (fat-free
   works just fine)**
½ cup uncooked brown and wild rice mix
½ cup uncooked barley
1 teaspoon dried sage leaves
1 teaspoon dried thyme leaves
**½ cup raisins (soak them ahead of time in a cup of
   hot tap water, at least ten minutes, then drain)**
¼ cup chopped green onions or regular onions
(optional: 1 to 1½ cups cooked beef, diced)

Cook on stovetop, about 1 hour total.

In a medium saucepan, stir together the broth, dry rice mix, dry barley, sage and thyme. Bring mixture to a boil, then reduce heat to simmer and cook 35–40 minutes, until all liquid is absorbed. Stir in raisins and onions, and optional beef. Heat for another ten minutes, stirring occasionally; if the mixture starts to stick to the bottom of the pan, add a Tablespoon or two of water and stir.

••

Chef Amee's Gourmet Touch

Add the juice and zest of 1 lime and 2 sprigs of fresh parsley leaves, chopped, after rice mixture has been simmering for about 20 minutes.

••

Burgundy Beef with Mushrooms

This dish doesn't take very long (a little more than half an hour to cook), but it offers the appearance and aroma of a much more involved combination. When you've added in the soup to simmer, it's a good time to put water on to boil to prepare egg noodles; serve the beef in its mushroom sauce spooned over individual plates of the tender noodles.

1½ pounds sirloin steak, cut in 1-inch chunks
1 Tablespoon vegetable oil
1 cup (about 8 ounces) mushrooms, sliced
2 medium onions, chopped
1 cup dry red wine (Burgundy is best, but Merlot
    works, too)
1 (11- to 14-ounce) can mushroom soup, undiluted
1 (8-ounce) package medium egg noodles, uncooked

Cook on stovetop, about 40 minutes total.

In a large frying pan or Dutch oven, brown the steak chunks in the oil, for about 10 minutes. Turn off the burner. Remove the steak and keep it warm on a plate covered with a bowl; keep the pot with the remaining oil ready on the stove.

Add the mushrooms and onions to the pot and cook over medium-high heat until the onions start to become clear. Stir in the wine and simmer for ten minutes. Add the soup and bring the mixture to a boil. Add the steak back into the pot and heat it all through on medium, for another five minutes.

Prepare egg noodles. Spoon beef and sauce over noodles.

. . . .

Chef Amee's Gourmet Touch

When in Burgundy, eat like the Burgundians—add 1 to 2 teaspoons of dried or fresh tarragon leaves, the herb of France. This recipe could also use about 5 cloves of garlic finely chopped and added when cooking the steak.

. . . .

Savory Mexican Pie

Cornmeal adds just a hint of crunch to this tender, makes-itself pie-crust. Onions and sweet peppers join in for a little sweetness and a splash of red, green, orange and yellow. Hint: buy onions and peppers on sale, chop them up, and keep them in zip-bags in the freezer for fast meal preparations.

Beef filling:
½ pound ground beef
¼ cup chopped onion
½ cup chopped sweet bell peppers (green or other colors)
1 (14.5-ounce) can diced tomatoes, drained
½ teaspoon chili powder
1 cup shredded mild cheddar cheese, divided

Crust:
2 eggs
¾ cup all-purpose flour
½ teaspoon salt
⅓ cup milk
1 Tablespoon cornmeal

Preheat oven to 400 degrees. Bake for 25 to 30 minutes.

In a large frying pan, brown the beef with the onion, using a stiff spatula to chop the beef into a fine crumble; drain any grease. Stir in the peppers and cook until tender. Add diced tomatoes and chili powder; cook on medium heat about five minutes. Remove from heat and stir in ½ cup shredded cheese.

In a medium-sized bowl, with a whisk or spoon, beat together the eggs, flour, salt, milk and remaining ½ cup shredded cheese. Grease a 9" pie pan. Pour flour mixture into the pan and sprinkle it with the cornmeal. Spoon the meat mixture into the center of the batter, keeping it one inch from the edge. Bake at 400 degrees for 25 to 30 minutes, until crust is lightly browned. Makes 8 slices.

· ·

Chef Amee's Gourmet Touch

Add 1 teaspoon cumin and 1 can of mild diced chiles for a true Mexican flavor. Try 1 to 2 teaspoons of both garlic powder and Mexican oregano in the crust mixture.

· ·

Corned Beef Casserole

Pam says she feels like a character in an Agatha Christie novel when she opens a "tin" of corned beef for this recipe. The ingredients mix together quickly and make a very filling dinner on a cool evening. Try serving the casserole with petite whole green beans from the freezer; they sometimes go by their French name, *petits haricots verts*.

1 (8-ounce) package medium egg noodles, uncooked
1 (12-ounce) can corned beef
1 (10½- to 14-ounce) can cream of celery soup, undiluted
¾ cup milk (use just ½ cup if using larger soup can)
1 Tablespoon dried minced onion
¼ cup bread crumbs (seasoned or toasted plain)

Preheat oven to 350 degrees. Bake for 30 minutes.

In saucepan, cook the noodles just until tender; drain. In a large bowl, chop the corned beef into a coarse crumbly texture. Stir in soup, milk and onion.

Grease a 2-quart casserole. Add the noodles and the corned beef mixture and stir together well. Sprinkle the bread crumbs on top. Bake covered at 350 degrees for 30 minutes. Serves 6 to 8 people.

Note: Freezes well. Try adding 2 Tablespoons water and ½ cup dry red wine when you reheat it on the stove or in the oven.

··

Chef Amee's Gourmet Touch

Add 1 cup of finely chopped purple cabbage, ¼ cup diced onion and 2 teaspoons fennel seed or powder for some true Irish flavor.

··

Brazilian Espresso Pot Roast

With this recipe for a stovetop simmered chuck roast, enjoying beef does not have to be a distant memory during your time in braces. The secret ingredient is strong coffee, which tenderizes the roast while imparting a simply delicious (non-coffee) flavor.

1 Tablespoon vegetable or olive oil
2½ to 3 pounds beef chuck roast
1½ cups strong coffee (regular or decaffeinated)
1 to 2 teaspoons chopped garlic
1 teaspoon salt
1 teaspoon ground thyme leaves
3 medium onions, peeled and sliced
6 small red potatoes, scrubbed and quartered
1 to 1½ cups water
(optional: ¼ cup flour and ½ cup water for gravy)

Cook on stovetop, about 2 hours total.

In a Dutch oven, pour the vegetable or olive oil to coat the bottom, and add the roast. Brown the roast on medium-high heat on both sides, as well as on the edges if you can manage it. Pour in the coffee and add the garlic, salt and thyme. Add onion slices. Cook over medium-high heat until liquid is boiling, then reduce heat to medium-low and simmer, covered, for 1 hour.

Add the potatoes and another 1½ to 2½ cups water, to make sure potatoes will be covered in liquid. Cover and cook another 45 minutes to 1 hour, until meat and potatoes are fork-tender.

If you'd like to make gravy, put the roast, potatoes and onions on a platter and keep them warm. In a small bowl, whisk together the flour and ½ cup water until all lumps are gone. Stir flour mixture into the pot of beef juices and cook on medium heat until thickened, 5 to 8 minutes. Serves 6 to 8 people.

••

Chef Amee's Gourmet Touch

Add 1 to 2 cups of baby carrots. I also recommend "deglazing" the roast with 1 cup of an "earthy" red wine such as a Carmenere to absorb the flavors from the pan-drippings. This is done after the roast is nearly browned and before you add the coffee and seasonings.

••

Budapest Ground Beef

Paprika is a traditional seasoning in many Hungarian dishes, adding a deep red color and slightly sweet flavor. While you're browning the beef, use a stiff spatula to chop the meat into a crumble—the fine texture helps the tomato-wine combination tenderize the beef.

1 pound ground beef
1 medium onion, chopped
1 teaspoon chopped garlic
1 cup Merlot or other dry red wine
1 (6-ounce) can tomato paste
1 to 2 teaspoons paprika (Hungarian sweet paprika is great)
2 (10½-ounce) cans beef broth, undiluted
1 cup water
1 (8-ounce) package medium egg noodles, uncooked

Cook on stovetop, about 30 minutes total.

In a Dutch oven or large frying pan, brown the beef, onion and garlic, chopping finely, for about 15 minutes. Stir in the wine, tomato paste and paprika; simmer on low for 5 minutes. Add beef broth, water and dry noodles; cover and bring the mixture to a boil. Reduce heat to medium-low and cook another 5 minutes or until noodles are tender. Serves 4 to 6 people.

••

Chef Amee's Gourmet Touch

Add 1 cup finely chopped mushrooms, 1 teaspoon dried mustard and a nice dollop of sour cream at the end. Simmer an additional 5 minutes. The sour cream gives the classic Hungarian taste.

••

Meatloaf in a Pumpkin/Squash

In the fall this makes an easy yet impressive main dish complete with its own side vegetable. Serve as wedges of pumpkin-plus-beef. When pumpkins aren't in season, use several dark green acorn-squash sliced down the center—the deep orange insides form a dramatic contrast, and guests receive their own halves.

1 pumpkin, approximately 8 inches to 10 inches diameter,
    or 3 to 4 small acorn-squash
2 pounds ground sirloin (best for its low fat)
2 eggs
¾ cup ketchup
½ cup water
¼ cup dried minced onion
1½ cups bread crumbs (plain or seasoned)

For pumpkin, bake at 350 degrees for 1½ to 2 hours.

For acorn squash, bake at 350 degrees for 1 to 1¼ hours.

For a pumpkin, cut out a "lid" about 5" diameter, then clean out and throw away the lid, seeds and stringy parts. For the squash, poke the sides of the squash three or four times with a fork, then microwave them uncut for 10 minutes on high power. This trick makes them much easier to cut and scoop. Using a hot-mitt to handle them, cut them in half, and clean out the seeds and strings.

In a large bowl, stir together the ground sirloin, eggs, ketchup, water and onion. Add bread crumbs and mix thoroughly. With a large spoon, scoop the meatloaf mixture into the pumpkin or squash-halves, filling just about to the brim. Put any leftover meatloaf in a 5" x 9" bread pan to bake by itself. Place pumpkin/squash in a 9" x 13" pan and pour in about half-an-inch of water in the bottom of the pan to keep the skins from burning. (Six squash-halves fit best into two 9" x 13" pans.) Bake at 350 degrees: the pumpkin will take 1½ to 2 hours, and squash-halves about 1 to 1¼ hours. A pan of extra meatloaf will usually take less time; check it at one hour. Serves 6 to 8.

••

Chef Amee's Gourmet Touch

Replace ketchup with 1 cup diced tomatoes, drained, plus 1 to 2 tea-spoons of sugar and 1 Tablespoon of chopped parsley leaves.

••

Beef Crumble Sandwiches

Up and down the Mississippi River, at homes, restaurants, and church picnics, you'll find some variation of this beef mixture spread between the halves of a hefty bun. Great for the days when even a hamburger would give you pause, this sandwich just may become a regular on your own menu. Some people enjoy it with a beer, others mix the beer right in with the beef; now there's food for thought.

1 pound ground beef
1 teaspoon chopped garlic
1 Tablespoon dried minced onion
1 (10¾-ounce) can chicken gumbo soup, undiluted
1 teaspoon salt
½ cup bread crumbs
4 sandwich buns
(optional: ketchup)

Cook on stovetop, about 20 minutes total.

In a large frying pan, brown the beef with the garlic and onion, chopping it to a fine crumble (the tool called a fish spatula is great for this task). Drain if necessary. Stir in the soup, salt and bread crumbs; simmer mixture for 5 minutes. Cut open the sandwich buns and spread one quarter of the mixture on each one. Add ketchup if desired. Serves 4.

For a variation, replace the soup with ½ cup tomato juice or sauce, whichever you have on hand, or ½ to 1 cup beer, plus ketchup to taste. Let it simmer to the thickness you prefer.

••

Chef Amee's Gourmet Touch

Add one can chopped mild green chiles to the beef mixture and top crumbled beef sandwich with a slice of Monterey Jack cheese for a bit of Southwest flair.

••

Parmesan Chicken Tenders

Restaurants and grocery stores sell a small portion of chicken strips for a premium price. You can create the same tender taste at home for a lot less money and with just a few ingredients. The simple coating seals in the moisture and sets you up for some great dipping options.

1½ pounds boneless chicken breasts (depending on size, this could be 2 to 4 halves)
2 egg whites
2 Tablespoons water
¾ to 1 cup seasoned dry bread crumbs
¼ cup Parmesan cheese, finely grated

Preheat oven to 400 degrees. Bake for 30 minutes.

Rinse the chicken and cut into strips about ¾" wide by 3" long. In a small bowl, whisk or stir together the egg whites and water. In a medium-sized bowl, stir together the bread crumbs and Parmesan cheese.

By hand or with a fork, dip each chicken strip into the egg-white mixture, then roll it in the bread-crumb mixture until evenly coated. You can do about 10 at a time.

Oil or grease a 9" x 13" pan. Lay the strips side by side in the pan and bake uncovered at 375 degrees for 20 minutes; turn the tenders over and bake 10 more minutes or until fork-tender. Serves 4 to 6 people.

• •

Chef Amee's Gourmet Touch

Add 1 Tablespoon dried Italian herbs to the bread crumb mixture. I would also recommend making a sweet Asian garlic dipping sauce using ½ cup of sweet chile and garlic sauce and 1 teaspoon of both minced ginger and spicy mustard.

• •

Apricot Chicken and Stuffing

A fragrant mixture of premixed herbs provides all the necessary seasonings when you use a bag of stuffing mix. Featuring boneless chicken breasts and apricot jam, this simple combination is the kind of recipe that takes care of itself in the oven then displays beautifully at the table. Prepare it in a glass pan for an extraordinary presentation.

3 boneless chicken breast halves, cut in half again
4 cups dry seasoned stuffing (the bagged kind)
2 to 2¾ cups chicken broth
½ cup apricot jam

Preheat oven to 350 degrees. Bake for 1¼ hours.

In a 9" x 13" greased pan (the greasing step really helps), stir together the dry stuffing with 2 cups of chicken broth; if your brand of stuffing seems dry, add up to ¾ cup more broth—you want it moist but not soggy. Spread the stuffing mixture evenly in the pan.

Lay the chicken breasts on top of the stuffing, and spoon a large Tablespoonful of apricot jam on top of each. Use the back of the spoon to spread the jam to thinly coat the chicken.

Cover the pan with foil and bake the chicken at 350 degrees for 1 hour or until tender. Remove the foil and bake an additional 5 minutes for a golden-brown touch. Serves 6.

....

Chef Amee's Gourmet Touch

Add ⅓ cup finely chopped dried apricots to the stuffing plus 2 chopped green onions and 1 teaspoon of minced ginger. It would also give it an Asian flair by drizzling a little sesame oil atop each chicken breast.

....

Hunter's Savory Chicken

Tomatoes serve as the tenderizing ingredient in this fragrant chicken-in-a-pot dish. With its onions, seasonings, tomatoes and wine, the mixture is a type of cacciatora (the Italian word for hunter). Make it in a slow cooker or a Dutch oven; if you have time to cut the boneless chicken into chunks first, they will absorb even more of the wonderful flavors.

3 to 4 boneless skinless chicken breast halves (best
    when cut in 2-inch chunks)
2 green peppers, diced
2 onions, cut in thick slices
1 (15-ounce) can dark red kidney beans, drained
1 (26-ounce) can or jar of tomato-based pasta
    sauce (any flavor)
1 cup dry red wine (Merlot or Burgundy work well)

Cooks on stovetop, 2 to 3 hours total.

Stir all ingredients together in a Dutch oven or slow cooker. Cover. For the Dutch oven, bring ingredients to a boil then simmer (slightly bubbling) for 1½ to 2 hours. For the slow cooker, allow at least three hours on medium. Check that the chicken is fork tender.

Try serving this dish with whole green beans and orzo pasta cooked in chicken broth. Serves 6 to 8 people.

··

Chef Amee's Gourmet Touch

Add 1 to 2 teaspoons of both dried mustard and dried rosemary. Serve it with one of my favorite accompaniments—short-grained brown rice.

··

Curried (No Cashew) Chicken

For a great curry recipe, you can usually ask someone British: they undoubtedly grew up on many dinners featuring the curry family of spicy seasonings. Pam turned to her Liverpudlian friend, Laura Garvie, for this fragrant oven-baked dish. It uses cooked chicken for a tender head start; when your braces come off, add cashews on top before baking.

2 Tablespoons vegetable or olive oil
3 large onions, chopped
1 to 3 Tablespoons curry powder (your choice)
1 cup plain yogurt or low-fat sour cream
1 teaspoon all-purpose flour
1 cup chicken broth
2 Tablespoons tomato paste
2 teaspoons lemon juice
½ to 1 teaspoon salt, as desired
3 cups (2 to 3 breast halves) cooked chicken, chopped

Preheat oven to 350 degrees. Bake for 30 minutes.

In a large frying pan or Dutch oven, heat the oil and cook the onions until they are very soft and lightly browned. Add the curry powder and continue to cook, stirring for 2 to 3 minutes. Remove from heat and add yogurt, flour, chicken broth, tomato paste, lemon juice and salt. Stir well.

Grease a 2-quart casserole. Spread chicken on the bottom, then pour sauce all over. Cover and bake at 350 degrees for 30 minutes. Serves 6 to 8 people.

Note: Curry seasonings can stain your ligatures (elastics)! Consider preparing this dish just before it's time to switch to new ones.

....

Chef Amee's Gourmet Touch

Add ⅓ cup diced red onion and ⅓ cup finely chopped peanuts for a more full-bodied flavor. The peanuts will soften as they bake.

....

Cranberry Glazed Chicken

Cranberries needn't be a holiday-time-only side-dish. Bring them into the spotlight with this easy glazed chicken and rice combination that uses two forms of cranberries: dried berries and whole-berry sauce. Prepare this recipe in a glass baking dish, and you'll be all set for company.

1½ cups mixed rice (white, brown, wild), uncooked
1 teaspoon dried thyme leaves
1 teaspoon dried basil
1 Tablespoon dried minced onion
2 cups chicken broth
¼ cup dried cranberries
3 boneless chicken breast halves
1 (16-ounce) can whole-berry cranberry sauce
¼ cup apple juice or cider

Preheat oven to 350 degrees. Bake for 1¼ to 1½ hours.

In a 9" x 13" greased baking dish, stir together the dry rice, thyme, basil and onion. Mix in the chicken broth and dried cranberries. Cut the chicken breasts into strips about 2 inches by 4 inches; this helps the flavor and moisture get absorbed so the chicken becomes very tender. Lay the chicken strips over the rice in a single layer.

In a medium-sized bowl, stir together the whole-cranberry sauce and apple juice. Pour the cranberry-juice mixture over all the chicken breast pieces.

Cover the pan tightly with foil, and bake at 350 degrees for 60 minutes. Remove the foil and bake for an additional 15 minutes, or until the chicken is very fork-tender. Serves 4 to 6 people.

....

Chef Amee's Gourmet Touch

Add one finely chopped shallot and replace the dried cranberries with ½ cup fresh cranberries.

....

Chicken Marsala with Noodles

If you've never tried cooking with Marsala wine, you are in for a treat. Slightly nutty, slightly sweet, this wine imparts a unique flavor that morphs into marvelous with stovetop simmering. Traditional Marsala recipes call for heavy cream, but this one works well just with a little milk.

1½ pounds boneless, skinless chicken breasts
  (2 to 3 halves)
3 Tablespoons flour (divided)
½ teaspoon dried oregano
½ teaspoon salt
Pepper to taste
2 Tablespoons olive or vegetable oil
1 teaspoon chopped garlic
1 medium onion, chopped
1 teaspoon dried thyme leaves
2 cups (about 4 to 5 ounces) small mushrooms, chopped
  into ½-inch bits (Baby Bella brown are great)
1 cup Marsala wine
2 Tablespoons butter
¼ cup milk
1 (8-ounce) package medium egg noodles, uncooked

Using kitchen shears or knife, cut the chicken into strips about 1 inch wide and 2 inches long. In a medium bowl, stir together 2 Tablespoons of flour, oregano, salt and pepper. Drop in chicken pieces to coat with flour mixture; discard extra flour. Place chicken in a large pot or skillet with a cover. Add the oil, garlic and onion, and cook on medium-high until the outsides of the strips are completely white, for about 10 minutes.

Stir in the thyme, mushrooms, wine and butter. Simmer covered for 10 minutes. Pour milk and 1 Tablespoon flour over the chicken mixture, stir together, and heat through uncovered on medium, 10 to 15 minutes to concentrate the sauce. Prepare the egg noodles according to directions. Spoon the chicken Marsala on top. Serves 4 to 6.

....

Chef Amee's Gourmet Touch

Replace the milk with ⅓ cup heavy cream; add the juice and zest of one lemon plus 8–10 finely chopped basil leaves. Instead of egg noodles, try using my favorite bowtie pasta noodles.

....

Creamed Chicken Puffs

This recipe makes a fantastic presentation for a fancy dinner, yet with a little beforehand preparation, it comes together quickly in two steps. Try preparing the cooked chicken ahead of time in a slow cooker (Pam's favorite cooking tool).

Puffs
- ½ cup water
- ¼ cup margarine or butter
- ¼ teaspoon salt
- (optional: ¼ teaspoon garlic powder)
- ½ cup all-purpose flour
- 2 eggs

Chicken Filling
- ¼ cup margarine or butter
- ¼ cup plus 2 Tablespoons Bisquick® or other mix
- ¼ teaspoon ginger
- 1 teaspoon chopped garlic
- 1 (14-ounce) can chicken broth
- ¼ cup water
- 1 Tablespoon lemon juice
- 1 cup frozen chopped broccoli, cooked
- 2 cups cooked chicken, cut up in small pieces

Preheat oven to 375 degrees. Total baking time 40 minutes.

For the puffs: in a medium saucepan, boil the water, margarine, salt and garlic. Stir in flour completely; remove from heat and allow to cool a few minutes. Beat in eggs vigorously until dough is well mixed and slightly stretchy. On a greased cookie sheet, spoon large Tablespoons of dough into 8 circles. Bake at 375 degrees until browned, about 40 minutes. Slit each puff into top and bottom halves.

While the puffs bake, in a large saucepan, melt the margarine and stir in the biscuit mix, ginger and garlic. Cook over low heat until smooth and bubbling, stirring constantly. Add chicken broth, water and lemon juice; boil for 1 minute and then reduce heat to medium. Stir in broccoli and chicken; heat for five minutes. Put two puff halves on each plate. Spoon on filling; replace the top halves. Serves 4.

. . . .

Chef Amee's Gourmet Touch

Serve with a dry, white wine such as Chardonnay or pinot grigio.

. . . .

Shrimp and Vegetable Stir-Fry

Talk about elegant. This shrimp stir-fry is easy to assemble yet looks extremely posh nestled into individual iceberg lettuce leaves or served with a mound of hot brown or jasmine rice. The lettuce provides a satisfying, braces-friendly crunch.

2 cups asparagus or broccoli, chopped (the frozen
    packaged type works well)
Water for boiling asparagus or broccoli
2 teaspoons lemon juice
1 teaspoon sugar
2 teaspoons soy sauce
2 teaspoons wine vinegar
4 teaspoons cornstarch
1 pound peeled cooked shrimp, de-tailed, coarsely chopped
2 Tablespoons vegetable or olive oil
3 teaspoons chopped garlic
1 Tablespoon chopped green onions
1 head iceberg lettuce

In a medium saucepan, add the lemon juice to the boiling water, and cook the asparagus or broccoli until tender (about 4 minutes). In a small bowl, whisk together the sugar, soy sauce, wine vinegar and cornstarch until smooth. Stir in the shrimp. Let the mixture marinate for 10 to 15 minutes.

In a large non-stick skillet, heat the 2 Tablespoons of oil and the garlic until sizzling. Pour the shrimp mixture with the marinade into the pan, and stir-fry the shrimp for about 3 minutes, just until it starts to turn orangey-pink. Add asparagus or broccoli and green onions.

Tear off large leaves from the head of lettuce and fill each with the shrimp mixture. Serves 4.

· ·

Chef Amee's Gourmet Touch

Add 1 teaspoon of fresh minced ginger and 4 cloves of chopped garlic to the sauce mixture. When cooking, use sesame oil instead of vegetable oil and splash some sweet chile and garlic sauce along with the sauce on top.

· ·

Seafood Melts

These open-faced sandwiches mix up very easily for a quick lunch or dinner and make a tender change from a burger-on-a-bun. The mild cheddar gives just a touch of tang, but you can experiment with other cheeses for a more robust flavor.

2 (6-ounce) cans tuna, drained
⅓ cup mayonnaise
1 Tablespoon dried minced onion
1 Tablespoon dried parsley
2 teaspoons lemon juice
¾ cup finely shredded mild cheddar cheese
4 English muffins, split in half

Broil for 3 to 4 minutes.

In a large bowl, stir together tuna, mayonnaise, onion, parsley, lemon juice and cheese.

Place the 8 muffin halves on a cookie sheet. Toast the tops lightly under the broiler, about 2 minutes. Remove from oven. Spread about 2 Tablespoons of the tuna mixture on top of each muffin half, all the way to the edges. Put cookie sheet under broiler an additional 3 to 4 minutes, until the cheese has melted a bit.

Serve immediately, or store in a covered container and reheat in the oven or microwave. Serve as finger-food, or, on particularly tender-teeth days, use a fork and knife to cut it into more manageable strips. Serves 4 people.

••

Chef Amee's Gourmet Touch

Replace cheddar cheese with Parmesan cheese and add 1 teaspoon of paprika. Serve this on top of a bed of arugula—my favorite green, leafy vegetable.

••

Anything-Goes Pasta Salad

A pasta salad can feature fruits, vegetables or both for a wonderful hot-weather entrée. Satisfy your craving for crunch by adding sliced water chestnuts; when your braces come off, add walnut pieces or sliced almonds. Plan on making it several hours ahead of time since it is best served chilled; this allows the flavors of herbs and dressings to mingle.

1 (8-ounce) package plain or multicolored shell or twist
    pasta, uncooked
¼ cup lemon juice
1 teaspoon dried basil
2 (11-ounce) cans mandarin oranges, drained
1 cup sugar-snap peas (cooked or raw), cut in halves
1 (8-ounce) can sliced water chestnuts
(optional: 1 (6-ounce) can crabmeat or tuna, drained)
3 Tablespoons olive oil or ¼ cup mayonnaise

Prepare pasta as directed and drain. Put pasta in a large bowl and stir in the lemon juice, basil, mandarin oranges, peas, water chestnuts, and optional crabmeat or tuna. Stir in your choice of olive oil or mayonnaise, and chill mixture for at least one hour.

· ·

Chef Amee's Gourmet Touch

Add 1 small can of finely chopped green or black olives and 8 finely chopped basil leaves for more color and a fuller flavor. Try replacing the expensive sugar snap peas with some frozen petite peas for a different look and taste.

· ·

Baked Tomato-Crab Pasta

This creamy tomato-pasta casserole is a variation on an old department-store recipe that was quite rich. In this version, instant mashed-potato flakes, milk and butter step in to create a simple, lower-fat substitute. Try serving it with peas.

2 cups small shell pasta, uncooked
½ cup chopped onion
2 Tablespoons butter or margarine
1 cup milk
¼ cup dry instant mashed-potato flakes
1 (10- to 14-ounce) can cream of tomato soup, undiluted
2 (6-ounce) cans crabmeat, drained
¼ cup grated Parmesan cheese
½ teaspoon dried ground marjoram

Preheat oven to 350 degrees. Bake for 30 minutes.

Grease a 3-quart casserole dish. In a large pot of boiling water, cook the pasta according to the package directions. While the pasta is cooking, use a large pot or saucepan to sauté the onions in the butter or margarine until they are clear.

Stir the milk and mashed-potato flakes into the onions and let the mixture bubble for 2 minutes on medium. Add the cream of tomato soup, crabmeat, Parmesan cheese and marjoram. Cook the mixture on medium another 5 minutes, then stir in the drained pasta.

Pour the crabmeat-pasta mixture into the casserole. If you'd like, sprinkle a little extra Parmesan cheese on top. Bake covered (to keep the top from getting crispy) at 350 degrees for 30 minutes. Serves 6 to 8.

···

Chef Amee's Gourmet Touch

Add half a chopped sweet bell pepper and 1 teaspoon of dried oregano to the crabmeat mixture. Serve this with a light, white wine such as a Sauvignon blanc.

···

Hummus and Tuna Grilled Sandwiches

Say goodbye to the mayonnaise and hello to hummus as the delectable partner for tuna in this hot griddle sandwich. Chopped spinach, handy from the freezer, provides a boost of color and nutrition.

2 (6-ounce) cans tuna, drained
1 cup plain hummus (purchased
   or homemade, see below)
¾ cup chopped spinach
   (if frozen, thaw in microwave)
½ teaspoon dried thyme leaves

6 slices multigrain bread
   (large slices)
½ cup milk
2 eggs
Vegetable oil for griddle

In a large bowl, stir together drained tuna, hummus, spinach and thyme. Spread the mixture on three slices of bread; cover with remaining slices. Press firmly together then cut them in half.

In a small bowl, beat together the milk and eggs. Pour the egg mixture into an 8" or 9" round or square pan to simplify dipping. Place each sandwich in the egg mixture, then with a fork and spatula, flip the sandwich so that both sides are well coated.

Pour a teaspoon or two of oil in a large frying pan or griddle, preferably one that can be covered. Heat the oil for a few minutes on medium, then add the sandwiches; cover if possible. You may have to cook them in two batches. Brown each side thoroughly for 5 or 6 minutes a side; be sure egg mixture looks cooked. Serve hot.

· ·

Chef Amee's Hummus:

¼ cup sesame oil
¼ cup vegetable or canola oil
2 Tablespoons lemon juice
2 cloves garlic, peeled
Salt and pepper to taste

1 (15 to 16-ounce) can
   garbanzo beans or
   chickpeas, drained
1 handful fresh parsley
   leaves

In a blender, combine oils and lemon juice. Add garlic, beans, parsley and seasonings. Blend until smooth.

· ·

Simple Salmon Patties

Pam keeps canned salmon on hand at all times because this recipe is easy to fix, soft for a tender-teeth night, and reheats well for a take-along lunch. She's partial to serving them with classic ketchup, but you might like to try tartar sauce or chutney.

1 (14.75-ounce) can pink or red salmon, drained
10 saltine crackers or round, buttery crackers
2 eggs
1 to 2 Tablespoons dried chives or 1 green onion,
**   finely chopped**
2 Tablespoons vegetable oil

Cook on stovetop, about 15 minutes total.

Place the salmon in a large bowl. Use a fork to remove all the round bones and break the fish sections into very small flakes. By hand, crumble the crackers into the bowl, breaking them into pea-sized pieces; stir the salmon and crackers together until very well combined.

Add the eggs and chives, and stir together thoroughly so that no egg is showing. Shape the salmon into six patties.

In a large, no-stick frying pan, heat the oil until it starts to sizzle. Place the patties carefully into the pan and brown them well, turning them once. (Cook patties at least 5 minutes on each side to be sure the egg is well-cooked.) Serves 6.

··

Chef Amee's Gourmet Touch

These yummy salmon patties make a great presentation and offer even more nutrients when served over a mound of whole wheat couscous.

··

Sausage and Chicken Paella

Paella may be the ultimate in customizable party dishes. Originally from Valencia, Spain, those in the know say it was a laborer's dish, cooked from leftovers on an open fire in the fields. There are hundreds of variations, including South American versions, so feel free to experiment. It feeds a crowd, it's a great way to combine your favorite vegetables, and the slow-simmered preparation tenderizes your choice of sausage, tiny shrimp, or shredded chicken. Though it does take three pans, most of the preparation is simultaneous, so you can fix it in about an hour.

1 cup dry rice
3 cups chopped broccoli
1 cup peas
1 Tablespoon vegetable or olive oil
10 small breakfast-link sausages
2 medium onions, chopped
1 cup sweet bell peppers, finely chopped
2 teaspoons chopped garlic
1½ cups sun-dried tomatoes, snipped into small pieces
1 (14-ounce) can chicken or vegetable broth
½ teaspoon salt
1 (14.5-ounce) can diced tomatoes, undrained
1 cup cooked, shredded chicken,
    or 1 (6-ounce) can cooked chicken
¼ cup (or ½ stalk) chopped celery
(optional: about 8 ounces of small cooked shrimp)

In one saucepan, start the rice cooking per package directions. In a second saucepan, cook the broccoli and peas.

Meanwhile, in a large pot or Dutch oven, brown the sausages in the oil and cut them in small pieces; add the onions, sweet peppers, garlic and sun-dried tomatoes, and cook until the onions are clear and the garlic lightly browned, about 15 minutes. Add the broth, salt, diced tomatoes, chicken, celery and shrimp; simmer over medium heat for 30 minutes. Stir in the rice and broccoli-pea mixture; simmer an additional 5 minutes.

••

Chef Amee's Gourmet Touch

Replace breakfast links with 1 pound of mild, ground chorizo and season with just a pinch of saffron for an authentic Spanish flavor.

••

Slow-Cooked Tomato Pork Roast

You'll find it hard to believe how something as simple as diced tomatoes makes this pork roast melt in your mouth. Whether you use a Dutch oven or a slow cooker, it's best to give it at least three hours of cooking. A meat thermometer is very handy and inexpensive for double-checking the cooking time. The roast will be safely done when it reaches 170 degrees, but as long as there's liquid in the pot, you can keep it simmering even longer.

2 pounds boneless pork roast, cut in two pieces
1 (14.5-ounce) can diced tomatoes, undrained
2 Tablespoons dried minced onion
2 teaspoons dried basil
½ teaspoon dried thyme leaves

Cook on stovetop, about 3 hours.

In a Dutch oven or slow cooker, place the two pork roast chunks (it cooks faster when cut in half this way). Add the diced tomatoes and sprinkle in the onion, basil and thyme. Cover and cook for at least three hours. For the Dutch oven, check the liquid level after about two hours; if there's very little left, add one cup of water.

Serve with couscous and your favorite green vegetable.

∙∙

Chef Amee's Gourmet Touch

Serve this hearty autumn dish with a loaf of freshly baked French bread (pick one up at the grocery store in the late afternoon) and a warm, red wine such as a Northwest coast pinot noir.

∙∙

Honey-Roasted Pork with Yams

A pork roast makes a truly succulent dinner, particularly when tenderized with a little lemon juice. This is a great dish for company, as the honey and brown sugar form a beautiful glaze and the vegetables get cooked at the same time. Try serving slices with a little side-dish surprise such as couscous (a tiny pasta), orzo, or the newly-popularized-yet-ancient grain called quinoa.

1 (3 to 4 pound) boneless pork tenderloin roast
Salt and pepper
2 Tablespoons all-purpose flour
¼ cup honey
¼ cup lemon juice
1 Tablespoon brown sugar
3 large yams, scrubbed and quartered
1 teaspoon dried rosemary
Salt and pepper to taste

Preheat oven to 375 degrees. Bake a total of 2¼ hours.

Cut the pork roast in half, fitting the two pieces easily into a 9" x 13" pan. Sprinkle flour on the tops, then turn them over and sprinkle more flour to cover all sides lightly. Bake at 375 degrees for 1 hour. Set the pan aside, but leave the oven on.

In a small bowl, stir together the honey, lemon juice and brown sugar. Place the yam quarters in the pan around the roast, then pour the honey sauce over the pork and the yams. Sprinkle pork with rosemary, salt and pepper. Bake for 45 minutes, cover the pan with foil, and bake another 30 minutes or until roast is done according to a meat thermometer.

···

Chef Amee's Gourmet Touch

Add the zest and juice of one orange when cooking the roast. Serve it with some fancy French green beans, haricots-verts, *for a lovely presentation.*

···

Vegetarian Ventures

Creamy Potato-Cheese Chowder

When the weather calls for a thick soup and fresh bread, stir up this quick chowder using instant potato flakes, blue cheese and mild cheddar. Based on milk, not cream (1% is just fine), it's even on the low-fat side.

3 Tablespoons butter or margarine
¾ cup chopped onion
½ cup chopped green sweet bell pepper
3½ cups milk
1 cup vegetable broth
1¼ cups dry instant mashed-potato flakes
¼ teaspoon dried thyme leaves
½ cup shredded mild cheddar cheese
2 Tablespoons blue cheese, crumbled

Cook on stovetop, about 20 minutes.

In a medium saucepan, cook the onion and green pepper in the butter until very soft, for about 10 minutes. Stir in the milk and vegetable broth and bring to a boil. Watch it closely, and turn the heat down to medium-low as soon as you see it start to boil. Add the potato flakes and thyme. Turn heat down to low, keep stirring and cook for 2 minutes until a bit thick.

Stir in the cheddar and blue cheeses until well melted and mixed, about 3 minutes. Serve immediately. Makes 4 servings.

···

Chef Amee's Gourmet Touch

For a creamier texture and flavor, replace potato flakes with 1½ cups frozen, shredded hash-browns and replace half of the milk with heavy whipping cream. To add a bit of a kick to this soup, replace the cheddar cheese with some shredded pepper jack cheese.

···

Cornbread Pizza

A pizza you can eat with a spoon? Served in squares, this dish is so different and yet so satisfying you'll love it when just the thought of dealing with a traditional pizza crust gives you pause. Stock your kitchen with pouches of grated cheese and boxes of cornbread mix, and you'll be ready to add whatever toppings strike your imagination.

2 (8½-ounce) boxes dry cornbread mix
2 eggs
1 cup milk
1 cup grated Parmesan cheese
1 jar or can (about 26 ounces) spaghetti sauce,
     any flavor
1 Tablespoon oregano
1 cup grated mozzarella cheese
Toppings of your choice, such as chopped green
     peppers, sliced mushrooms, olives and onions

Preheat oven to 375 degrees. Bake for 30 to 35 minutes total.

In a large bowl, stir together the 2 boxes of dry cornbread mix, 2 eggs, milk and Parmesan cheese. Grease a 9" x 13" pan, and also grease 6 muffin-pan cups (or line them with cupcake papers). Spoon batter into the 6 muffin cups, about halfway, as this is extra batter. (You'll have muffins for another meal—they're great with chili.) Then spread the remaining batter into the 9" x 13" pan and spread the spaghetti sauce over the top. Sprinkle with oregano.

Bake the pizza and the muffins at 375 degrees for 15 minutes and remove both from oven. Sprinkle the pizza with the mozzarella cheese and any other toppings, then bake it an additional 10 to 15 minutes. Cut into squares.

....

Chef Amee's Gourmet Touch

To make two specialty "soft" pizzas, bake them in two round cake pans and top with your favorite toppings. Add 1 Tablespoon of dried Italian herbs to the pizza crust along with 1 teaspoon of garlic powder for added flavor.

....

Roasted Eggplant Boats

This recipe has its roots in Greek and Turkish dishes made from eggplants, tomatoes and whatever spices are on hand. It has another, delightful name, *imam baldi,* which means literally, "the wise man fainted." Legend has it the dish was served to a visiting holy man, who found it so delicious he promptly fainted.

1 large eggplant
1 to 2 teaspoons salt (divided)
1 cup chopped onion
2 teaspoons chopped garlic
1 Tablespoon vegetable or olive oil
1 (14.5-ounce) can diced tomatoes, drained
1 teaspoon dried basil
1 teaspoon dried oregano
1 cup vegetable broth
(optional: ¼ cup feta cheese crumbles)

Preheat oven to 350 degrees. Bake for 1 hour total.

Grease a 9" x 13" pan. Cut the eggplant in half lengthwise (cut off stem). Scoop out (and keep) the insides, leaving about a ½-inch shell; a curved grapefruit knife works well for this task. Chop the eggplant chunks into half-inch bits and set aside. Place the halves facing up in the pan; sprinkle with ½ teaspoon salt and fill halfway with water. Pour ½ inch of water in the pan itself. Bake at 350 degrees for 30 minutes. Remove from oven and drain water from pan and eggplants; return eggplants to pan.

In the meantime, in a large frying pan or Dutch oven, cook the onion and garlic in the oil for 10 minutes. Stir in the tomatoes, eggplant-bits, basil, oregano, ½ teaspoon salt and broth. Simmer for 20 minutes. Fill eggplant halves with the tomato mixture; they will be mounded high. Bake for 30 minutes. Sprinkle with cheese, as desired and salt to taste.

••

Chef Amee's Gourmet Touch

Top this dish with your own Greek-style sauce using 1 cup plain Greek-style yogurt, ⅓ cup feta cheese, 1 cup diced cucumbers, and salt and pepper to taste.

••

Garden Bounty Casserole

You could call this a rice casserole with an awesome vegetable topping, or a great vegetable dish that makes its own rice. Either way, you can be inventive with whatever vegetables are on hand, and vary the flavor by using today's brown or wild-rice combinations. It comes together quickly if you keep chopped bags of onions, sweet peppers, broccoli and cauliflower in your freezer. (No need to thaw them.)

2 Tablespoons butter or margarine, melted
1½ cups rice, uncooked
2 cups chopped onions (divided)
3 cups vegetable broth
3 Tablespoons soy sauce
½ teaspoon dried thyme leaves
1 teaspoon salt
2 Tablespoons vegetable oil
1 teaspoon chopped garlic
1½ cups chopped broccoli
1½ cups chopped cauliflower
½ cup chopped sweet bell peppers, any color

Preheat oven to 350 degrees. Bake a total time of 70 minutes.

Grease a 3-quart casserole. Stir in butter, rice, 1 cup onions, broth, soy sauce, thyme and salt. Cover and bake at 350 degrees for 60 minutes.

In the meantime, in a frying pan or Dutch oven, heat the oil and add the garlic, 1 cup onions, broccoli, cauliflower and peppers. Heat on medium-high, stirring frequently, until garlic starts to brown, about 8 minutes.

Spread vegetable mixture over top of rice mixture. Cover and bake at 350 degrees for 10 minutes.

··

Chef Amee's Gourmet Touch

Replace traditional soy sauce with a peanut satay sauce found in many grocery stores, located in the Asian food section. Top this casserole with 1 cup of finely chopped peanuts. I know that peanuts and vegetables don't normally sound fabulous together, but this can prove 'em wrong.

··

Swiss Tomato Fondue

Ten minutes is all it takes to whip up this creamy, not-too-rich fondue. Serve it in a fondue pot and let guests dip the traditional long forks with chunks of French bread, crusts removed. The longer this mixture simmers in the pot, the more it creates the classic "croustine" layer at the bottom—some people vie for a spoonful of this golden prize. If you actually have leftovers, use the fondue as a soft spread on buttery crackers or pita bread for a quick and flavorful snack.

2 (14.5-ounce) cans diced tomatoes, well-drained
2 Tablespoons cornstarch
½ cup white wine
1 teaspoon dried basil
½ teaspoon salt
¾ pound Swiss cheese, cubed

In a medium saucepan, heat the tomatoes on medium high until boiling. Turn heat to medium. In a measuring cup, stir cornstarch into wine until dissolved. Add wine mixture, basil and salt to tomatoes; cook for 2 minutes. Turn heat to medium low. Add cheese cubes a few at a time, stirring constantly, until all cheese is melted, about 5 minutes. Transfer to fondue pot and keep warm for dipping.

Serves 4.

....

Chef Amee's Gourmet Touch

Add some fresh vegetables such as broccoli or cauliflower florettes and celery or carrot sticks for dipping. Also, try replacing the Swiss cheese with either cubed Gruyère or Emmanthaler cheese for even more Swiss authenticity. Serve it with a subtle yet sweet wine from Austria called Grüner Veltliner.

....

Sweet Onion Pie

If you love caramelized onions on anything (or just by the spoonful), this recipe is for you. When available, Vidalia, Texas 1015 and Walla Walla sweet onions are phenomenal, but regular yellow onions offer wonderful flavor, too. A packaged biscuit mix lets you whip up this pie in a flash and even makes its own semifirm crust. Serve it with a salad and fresh (soft) bread.

3 Tablespoons vegetable oil
2½ cups chopped onions
3 eggs
1½ cups milk
½ cup packaged biscuit mix (such as Bisquick®)
½ teaspoon salt
1 cup shredded Swiss cheese

Preheat oven to 350 degrees. Bake for 50 to 60 minutes.

In a large frying pan, stir-fry the onions in the vegetable oil over medium-high heat, until they are very limp and lightly browned (10 to 15 minutes). In a large bowl, whisk together the eggs, milk, biscuit mix and salt.

Grease a 9" or 10" pie pan. Pour in the egg mixture, and stir in the cheese and the onions along with any remaining oil.

Bake the 9" pan for 60 minutes at 350 degrees; bake the 10" pan for 50 minutes. Let stand 10 minutes before cutting. Serves 8.

....

Chef Amee's Gourmet Touch

Add 1 teaspoon of both dried tarragon and freshly ground nutmeg, and replace the Swiss cheese with a more refined and pungent cheese, Gruyère. I also recommend cooking the onions with a dry, white wine such as a Chardonnay.

....

Homemade Polenta with Mushroom Glaze

Cornmeal is an often overlooked ingredient that adds unusual texture and flavor. This recipe creates a light and fluffy version of a traditional cornmeal-based Italian dish called polenta. It works well as a more robust alternative to mashed potatoes or pasta. The tomato-mushroom combination simmers down to a dark, intense sauce for a rich-looking presentation.

1 Tablespoon olive oil
1 teaspoon chopped garlic
8 ounces (about 2 cups) mushrooms, thinly chopped (Baby
    Bellas or other brown mushrooms are a great choice)
1 cup vegetable broth
1 (8-ounce) can tomato sauce
1 teaspoon salt (divided)
½ teaspoon dried rosemary
1 teaspoon dried basil
2½ cups water (divided)
1 cup dry cornmeal
½ teaspoon dried oregano
(optional: ½ cup grated cheese such as Colby jack)

Cooks on stovetop, about 40 minutes total.

In a large frying pan or Dutch oven, heat the olive oil over medium-high and add the garlic; cook about 2 minutes until garlic starts to brown. Add the mushrooms and broth and bring mixture to a boil. Cover and simmer for 5 minutes. Stir in the tomato sauce, ¼ teaspoon salt, rosemary and basil. Simmer for 15 minutes, then keep mixture warm.

In a medium saucepan, boil 1½ cups water, add ¾ teaspoon salt, and turn heat to simmer. In a medium-sized bowl, stir together cornmeal, oregano and 1 cup water; let mixture sit 2 minutes while it thickens. Stir the cornmeal mixture slowly into the saucepan of water; keep stirring and cooking for 6 to 7 minutes so that mixture thickens. Stir in cheese; spoon onto serving plate. Pour on mushroom sauce. Serves 4.

••

Chef Amee's Gourmet Touch

Serve this dish with a grilled white fish such as tilapia or flounder and pair it with a light green salad of arugula and spinach.

••

Delicate Desserts

Pumpkin Chocolate-Chip Softies

Mmmm—nutmeg, cinnamon and ginger—enjoy the fragrance of Thanksgiving cooking without all the fuss. These cookies combine the moisture of pumpkin purée and the fun of chocolate chips. They're even softer the second day (if you can wait that long), after they've been placed in a tightly sealed container.

1⅓ cups all-purpose flour
1 teaspoon baking powder
½ teaspoon baking soda
½ teaspoon salt
1 teaspoon cinnamon
½ teaspoon ground ginger
½ teaspoon nutmeg
1 (15-ounce) can plain pumpkin purée
¾ cup light brown sugar, packed
2 eggs
¼ vegetable oil
2 Tablespoons molasses
1 Tablespoon milk
1 (12-ounce) bag chocolate chips

Preheat oven to 350 degrees. Bake for 25 minutes.

In a medium-sized mixing bowl, stir together the flour, baking powder, baking soda, salt, cinnamon, ginger and nutmeg. In a large mixing bowl, with a mixer or whisk, combine the pumpkin, brown sugar, eggs, oil, molasses and milk. Add the flour mixture slowly into the pumpkin mixture until well combined. Stir in the chocolate chips.

The dough is very soft. Drop by heaping Tablespoons onto greased cookie sheets, 12 cookies to a pan. Bake at 350 degrees for 25 minutes. Makes 36–40 cookies. Store in a covered container between sheets of waxed paper.

....

Chef Amee's Gourmet Touch

Replace all-purpose flour with my favorite secret baking ingredient— whole-wheat pastry flour, about 1¼ cups. Not only is it healthier, but it keeps baked goods moist longer. Top these little cookies with a sprinkle of fine sugar for a bit of added sparkle, and bake according to directions.

....

Dark Vanilla Drops

These thick, round mounds are not your ordinary butter or sugar cookies. Brown sugar makes them dark, and an unusual three teaspoons of vanilla makes them intense. Keep them in a tightly-covered container to maintain their soft texture. The dough freezes well, so you can bake one panful and keep the rest for later; just defrost on the counter for an hour or so.

½ cup butter or margarine, softened
¼ cup white sugar
¾ cup brown sugar
2 eggs
3 teaspoons vanilla
2 cups all-purpose flour
1 teaspoon baking soda
1 teaspoon salt

Preheat oven to 375 degrees. Bake for 9 minutes.

In a large bowl, cream together the butter and both sugars with a mixer. Add eggs and vanilla, then mix in flour, baking soda and salt until well combined. Dough will be rather stiff.

Drop by rounded Tablespoons onto ungreased cookie sheets. Bake at 375 degrees for 9 minutes. Store in a covered container. Makes 3 dozen.

....

Chef Amee's Gourmet Touch

Drizzle ½ cup melted chocolate chips over cookies after baking. This will keep you in the good graces of adults who can't understand how you can make a decent cookie just using vanilla.

....

Mandarin Orange Cake

You don't often find a dessert that uses mandarin oranges, but those juicy little slices bring an exotic flavor to this brown-sugar-laced cake. Extra special when served hot, this recipe features a sponge-cake-like texture that's easy on tender teeth and keeps fresh for days. Just cover the 9" x 13" pan with foil.

1½ cups sugar
2 cups all-purpose flour
2 teaspoons baking soda
½ teaspoon salt
2 eggs
2 (11-ounce) cans mandarin oranges, drained (do not
    use the liquid)

Sugar icing:
    ¾ cup brown sugar, packed
    3 Tablespoons milk
    2 Tablespoons butter or margarine

Preheat oven to 350 degrees. Bake for 30 to 35 minutes.

In a large bowl, stir together the sugar, flour, baking soda and salt. With an electric mixer, add eggs and drained mandarin oranges, and beat for 4 minutes.

Grease a 9" x 13" pan. Pour in batter. Bake at 350 degrees for 30 to 35 minutes, or until cake springs back when the center is touched.

In a medium-sized saucepan, stir together the brown sugar, milk and butter or margarine. Bring to a boil, stirring well until all ingredients are combined and bubbling. Remove from heat. Pour sugar icing over cake while cake is still hot. Smooth icing on evenly with a knife.

· ·

Chef Amee's Gourmet Touch

Add the zest of one orange to the cake batter. Add ½ teaspoon almond extract to the sugar icing for a richer flavor. Top with mandarin orange slices for a gorgeous presentation.

· ·

Almond Buttery Bars

Credit for this marzipan-like concoction goes to family friend Laura Hurtig, who loves to invent new recipes, even though she's immersed in business school and doesn't actually wear braces. These bars sport a melt-in-your-mouth texture somewhat like classic fudge and get their rich flavor from equal amounts of oil and real butter.

1½ cups sugar
⅔ cup butter, softened (not margarine)
½ cup vegetable oil
2 Tablespoons milk
1½ Tablespoons pure almond extract (yes, Tablespoons)
2 eggs
3 cups all-purpose flour
3 teaspoons baking powder
¼ teaspoon salt

Preheat oven to 375 degrees. Bake for 12 minutes.

In a large bowl, with an electric mixer, combine the sugar, butter and oil. Add milk, almond extract and eggs. Slowly add flour, baking powder and salt; dough will get quite stiff. If you have a hand mixer, you may need to finish up by switching to stirring with a large spoon.

Spread the dough evenly into an ungreased 9" x 13" pan. Bake at 375 degrees for 12 minutes. These seem quite rich, so cut them into 64 small bars—great for a party.

....

Chef Amee's Gourmet Touch

Make a simple topping for these delicate bars by combining ½ cup finely chopped almonds, 2 Tablespoons of sugar and ¼ teaspoon freshly ground nutmeg. Sprinkle on top before baking.

....

Strawberries and Cream Slush Drink

Chef Amee created this grown-up version of a summertime favorite, whipped up in minutes with a blender. You can use either fresh or frozen strawberries. Adjust the sugar to your liking.

2½ cups (about 1 pound) strawberries, fresh or frozen
1 Tablespoon lime juice
1½ cups crushed ice
1½ cups club soda
3 Tablespoons vanilla syrup (sold as a coffee flavoring)
½ cup sugar or more, to taste
1 can whipped cream

Wash and drain strawberries. Remove stems and slice. Put lime juice in blender, then add batches of strawberries, about a half-cup at a time, blending until liquefied. Strain the strawberries through a fine sieve to remove most of the seeds and some pulp. Place back in blender, and blend with the crushed ice. Pour into a 2-liter pitcher and stir in club soda, vanilla syrup and sugar. Serve in six tall glasses with a swish of whipped cream on top.

Chef Amee's Watermelon Sorbet

¾ cup water
¼ cup sugar
1 teaspoon lime juice
2 to 3 cups watermelon, diced, no seeds or rind

In a small saucepan, heat the water, sugar and lime juice on medium-high for 1 to 2 minutes, stirring until the sugar has dissolved. Chill this "syrup" at least 20 minutes. In the meantime, place the watermelon chunks in a food processor or blender and liquefy them. Add the chilled syrup to the watermelon puree and blend. Freeze sorbet in an ice-cream maker according to manufacturer's directions. Serve immediately for best flavor.

Websites of Interest

www.BracesCookbook.com
Visit often for new ideas. Discover more great tips, trivia and recipes (especially desserts!) by ordering the award-winning original book, **The Braces Cookbook: Recipes You (and Your Orthodontist) Will Love**.

* * * *

www.ada.org/public/topics/braces_faq.asp
Presented by the American Dental Association, this website provides a serious and informative discussion about braces and orthodontics.

www.agd.org/public/oralhealth/
Part of the website of the Academy of General Dentistry, this site offers helpful information, particularly for adult braces-wearers. Click on the Orthodontics sections.

www.archwired.com
This is **the** interactive website for adults in braces. Read the Q&A sections for great advice from experienced braces-wearers, and post your own forum-questions.

www.bracesinfo.com
A little bit dated, this site still covers almost everything you ever wanted to know about braces.

www.braces.org
The American Association of Orthodontists hosts this consumer-friendly website, which includes articles, recipes, and answers to FAQs.

www.dentaltown.com
An international e-zine and dental community with professional discussion boards, this site has categories covering more than eighty six topics, including orthodontics. Anyone can join and post questions.

www.dentakit.com
A terrific online store featuring handy products (including tiny spiral brushes) for anyone wearing braces, retainers, or aligners. Especially great ideas for work and travel.

www.pbhs.com/ortho/braces/braces.html
If you choose to wear colored elastics, this website lets you test the look of different color combinations.

Glossary of Orthodontic Terms

Unofficial and nonmedical, these descriptions should still be helpful as you proceed with your orthodontic treatment.

Aligners: clear removable pieces of slide-on plastic that cover your upper or lower teeth to shift them a bit; an alternative to some types of orthodontic treatment.

Arch wire: the U-shaped wire that connects all your brackets and does the main job of the braces treatment.

Band: a metal ring that is cemented all around a tooth, generally with a bracket on it that can hold an arch wire; usually placed on the back molar, or on a tooth with a gold crown.

Bracket: a small piece of metal, ceramic or plastic bonded to the front (traditional braces) or back (lingual braces) of a tooth; it has a slot to hold the arch wire in place.

Buccal tube: a small piece of hollow metal welded to a molar band; it can hold the end of an arch wire.

Chain: a stretchy, connected row of round elastics, used to hold each bracket to the arch wire. Sometimes called a power-chain.

Ligatures: proper name for the tiny individual elastics that hold the arch wire onto each bracket; latex versions come in dozens of colors. If you are allergic to latex, you will probably have clear or silver ligatures.

Lingual: the side of a tooth that faces the tongue.

Malocclusion: a Latin term meaning "bad bite," used to generally describe teeth that do not meet or fit together in the best possible way.

Mandible: the lower jaw.

Maxilla: the upper jaw.

Retainer: a fixed or removable device worn after bonded braces have been removed; it keeps the teeth in their final place. Wear it!!

Separators: tiny temporary elastic or metal rings slid between two teeth prior to getting braces, to create a little space for any metal bands. Generally used a few days or a week.

Wax: either real wax or silicon, used in tiny bits to temporarily cover a hook or bracket that is rubbing inside the mouth.

About the Authors

Pamela Waterman is an author, editor, engineer and member of a family with three generations of braces wearers. She enjoys hands-on projects in 3D art, cooking, building, and science.

Other books by Ms. Waterman include *The Braces Cookbook: Recipes You (and Your Orthodontist) Will Love*, *The Absolute Best Play Days: From Airplanes to Zoos (and Everything In Between)* and *JumpStart 5th Grade Activities*. Her articles on engineering, parenting, small business, and home renovation have appeared in such publications as *Desktop Engineering*, *Family Fun*, *Cricket*, *Highlights for Children*, and *Better Homes and Gardens Kids' Rooms*.

Chef Amee Hoge has a passion for equipping and inspiring young people and adults by teaching them how to play with food creatively in the kitchen. She graduated from Northern Arizona University with a bachelor's degree in elementary education, and has worked in a residential care facility in Missouri with at-risk youth, where her passion to reach these "tough" kids through cooking began. A graduate of the French Culinary Institute of New York City, she is currently living in Arizona and teaching classes to all ages. She is a regular guest chef on the *Arizona Midday Show*, a contributing writer for *Raising Arizona Kids* Magazine and a member of Women Chefs and Restaurateurs (WCR).

Index

Note: Page numbers in italics refer to photographs.

Give the gift of Comfort-Food Eating
to family, friends and patients

CHECK YOUR LOCAL BOOKSTORE OR ORDER HERE

_____ copies of **The Braces Cookbook** at $9.95 each plus $3.50 shipping for a total of $13.45. (Arizona residents please add $0.80 sales tax per book.)

_____ copies of **The Braces Cookbook 2** at $14.95 each plus $5.00 shipping for a total of $19.95. (Arizona residents please add $1.20 sales tax per book.)

_____ cartons of **The Braces Cookbook**, at 25 books/carton, at the professional discount cost of $125/carton plus $15.00 shipping/handling per carton. (Arizona residents please add $10.06 sales tax per carton.) **For Canada and other countries, please phone us for shipping costs.**

Canadian orders must be accompanied by a postal money order in U.S. currency value.

My check or money order to The Discovery Box for $ _____ is enclosed.

Name _____

Address _____

City/State/Zip _____

Phone _____ Email (optional) _____

Please remit check along with this form by mail to:

**Braces Cookbook Request
The Discovery Box
1955 W. Baseline Rd.
Ste. 113-234
Mesa AZ 85202**

Any questions? Call us at 480-897-3380
www.BracesCookbook.com